How to get Approved for a Mortgage the First Time

by

Dr. Melissa Weathersby

www.MelissaWeathersby.com

Dedication

This book is dedicated to all who are striving to make home ownership their reality. May you leave an inheritance to your children's children.

Table of Contents

There are three parts to the entire mortgage approval, but this book will focus on how you -as the borrower- can get approved the very first time you apply for your mortgage loan. Many borrowers suffer embarrassment or delay because they are not fully prepared when they speak to their mortgage loan officer to apply for their loan. This book will discuss, in depth, the underwriting process and how to get approved the very first time when applying for a home mortgage. We will focus on pleasing the underwriter who is the person that will approve or deny your loan request.

①②③
THE BORROWER →THE PROPERTY → THE TITLE DEED

There are three parts to the **mortgage approval process**. The first is you: the borrower! The second is the property that you're purchasing, and lastly, the title-or chain of ownership- to the property that you are purchasing. All three parts *must be* approved in order for the loan transaction to be approved. This book will only focus on the BORROWER's portion of the mortgage approval process. You won't have any input as to the property value or condition of the property title so our focus will be on making sure your portion of the mortgage approval process is approved **the first time** you apply!

The three parts to the borrower's portion of the mortgage approval process are: your *capacity* to repay the loan, your *credit history*, and the *collateral* that will be used to secure the loan. These 3 factors are the exact things an underwriter will examine before determining your eligibility for a home mortgage.

The underwriter asks these three questions when considering each and every borrower:

① Does this borrower have the CAPACITY (steady, reliable income) to repay this loan consistently and completely?

② Does this borrower have the

CHARACTER (credit history) to repay this loan consistently and completely? ③ Is the COLLATERAL (the property being purchased) sufficient to secure this mortgage in the event this borrower defaults on the mortgage contract?

The mortgage loan application is a very detailed document that asks very specific information about your income, employment, outstanding debt obligations, assets, and credit history. You _must_ be honest when answering the questions on your application or face being declined if any discrepancies are found during the verification process. If fraud is found in your application after you close on your mortgage, you may be asked to immediately pay the loan balance in full and/or pay penalties and fines or even face imprisonment. It's never worth it to lie on any loan application!

YOUR CAPACITY

The borrower's ability to make mortgage payments on time is called "capacity." The underwriter will examine factors that affect the borrower's capacity such as:

1) the borrower's income stability,

2) job history, and

3) job type.

Keep in mind that when the underwriter is looking at approving a mortgage application, a mortgage is a _**very**_ long-term commitment. A typical borrower is going to borrow the mortgage amount for no less than 15 years (180 months!), so the underwriter is going to scrutinize all parts of this mortgage file before authorizing the disbursement of hundreds of thousands or even millions of dollars. When looking at capacity, the debt to income ratio is utilized. Debt to income is the ratio that divides the amount of debt payments being paid out monthly by the amount of monthly income. "Before tax" income is used in this ratio. The lower the ratio, the better.

For example:

A borrower earns $60,000 annually and has one monthly car payment of $350 and one monthly credit card payment of $75.

$60,000/12= $5,000/month

$350+$75 = $425

Debt ratio: Monthly Debt payments/Gross monthly income

Debt ratio= .085 or 9%

The standard qualifying debt-to-income ratio underwriters use to qualify a borrower for conventional mortgage financing is **28%** of the borrower's **gross monthly income**. This number is your maximum **house payment** allowed. This house payment includes: the loan principal, loan interest, property taxes and property insurance, *as well as* any homeowner's association fees and private mortgage insurance premiums. This is known as "P.I.T.I." (Principal, Interest, Taxes, and Insurance + other monthly housing financing costs). FHA and VA loan programs have more relaxed guidelines.

The second ratio that the underwriter will look at when looking at capacity is your **overall** debt-to-income ratio, which includes the new house payment <u>and</u> all other monthly debts. It's also known as a "back-end ratio." Your monthly overall debt-to- income ratio cannot be more than **36%** of your gross monthly income. This ratio includes: your house payment PLUS all of your existing monthly payments (ex. your car payment, your student loan payments, credit card payments, child support payments, alimony or palimony payments, etc.).

EXAMPLE

Your annual income is $60,000.
You have a car payment of $175
and a credit card payment of $50.
How much house can you afford?

Using the conventional 28/36 ratios
(where 28% of gross monthly income= maximum allowable house payment and 36% of gross monthly income = total debt ratio including new house payment)
60,000/12 = $5,000/gross monthly income

$5,000*.28= \$1,400$ is the maximum allowable house payment (P.I.T.I.)

$5,000*.36= \$1,800$ is the maximum allowable <u>total</u> monthly debt, therefore, we must now subtract your debt payments to <u>verify</u> the maximum allowable house payment
$\$1,800-\$175$ (car payment)-$\$50$(credit card) = $\$1,575>\$1,400$

In this example, $1400 (28% of $5,000) is the maximum allowable <u>house payment</u> because conventional mortgage underwriting guidelines only allow a maximum 28% of the borrower's monthly income to be used for the house payment.

***BUT <u>WHAT IF</u>** there was also a student loan of $250?*

$1800 (maximum overall debt allowed)-$175(car payment) -$50(credit card)- $250 (student loan) = $1,325

Because the overall debt ratio <u>must</u> include all monthly debts PLUS the new house payment, the addition of the student loan reduces the maximum allowable house payment to $1,325 instead of $1,400.

<u>Therefore, the more debt you have, the less house you will qualify for.</u>

Your lender is also concerned with the

borrower's (your) cash reserves and whether the

borrower is a salaried employee or self-employed

worker. When qualifying the buyer, the mortgage

underwriter will determine your income and job

stability by reviewing two years of your

previously filed tax returns with the IRS. In

addition to your last two years of filed tax returns,

you will also need to submit your last two months

of bank statements showing cashflow, which

would be your direct deposits or if you are self-

employed, customer payments. Your bank

statements will also confirm your cash reserves available for the down payment and closing costs of the mortgage loan transaction. The underwriter is also looking to see if there are any negative issues going on in your bank account. If you have bounced checks or you are overdrawn, that typically will get your application declined. Before you turn your bank statements in to your loan officer, make sure that the down payment *and* closing costs are already in your savings account. A new deposit showing a large amount will be a red flag to an underwriter. If it is a gift for your home purchase, you will want to have a gift

> FHA qualifying ratios are 31% housing/43% debt ratio.
> VA only uses one ratio of 41% total debt ratio.

letter signed and verified by the giftor's bank to present along with your bank statements. This gift letter must explicitly state that the amount being gifted will not have to be repaid at any time for any reason. This amount must match the amount of the deposit into your account right down to the penny! Submit the gift letter at the time of application along with your bank statements and tax returns to increase your odds of getting approved quickly.

Another type of verification document that an underwriter will want to see when approving the **capacity** of the borrower will be your last two paystubs received from your employer showing a year-to-date balance. If you are self- employed, submit a certified, year-to-date, profit and loss statement showing revenue minus expenses along with bank statements and supporting income documents. Be sure to include certified bank statements for all accounts that you used to describe your assets on your loan application. This would be your checking account, your savings account, your 401k account, your investment accounts, etc. Keep in mind that although you are providing this documentation, your lender will also verify the documents that you have presented in order to validate your information. Any and all discrepancies between what you have presented and what the lender validates must be clearly documented and remedied, or your mortgage loan application will be declined. It is important that you have all of your paperwork in order and that it must be verifiable in order for you to be approved for your mortgage loan ***before you apply*** for the loan! You should understand how your debt-to-income ratio works and be sure that you can verify ***all*** of your employment within the last two years. Multiple jobs in short periods of time, not being able to verify employment, or gaps in employment are red flags to an underwriter and can potentially be reasons for declining you for a mortgage loan. A reasonable exception to this issue is if you are in an industry, and you are being promoted quickly, you can show that you are on a career path. But if you are going from job to job without any rhyme or reason, you will probably be declined for your loan. Stability is key for being approved for a mortgage loan. If you know your job history is spotty, do not apply. Wait until your capacity is solid.

YOUR CHARACTER

The next part of the mortgage process is CHARACTER: your credit history.

Credit seems to be one of the biggest obstacles that borrowers face. When applying for a mortgage loan, know that your **entire** credit and payment history will be heavily scrutinized. There are three credit repositories that the lender looks at. The three credit repositories, also called **credit bureaus**, are TransUnion, Experian, and Equifax. Each of these credit bureaus contain files of your entire credit history. Credit cards, department store accounts, gasoline accounts, any installment loans, student loans, and auto loans are all housed in one or all of these repositories, and they each will generate a credit score once enough payment history has been compiled. Judgments, bankruptcies, foreclosures, repossessions, evictions, charge-offs, utility company collection accounts and unpaid child support may also be reported to any or all three of these repositories. Not all creditors report to all three credit bureaus so your credit score will not be the same with each bureau. The Fair Isaac Corporation created a risk-analysis algorithm which measures consumer credit risk known as a FICO® Score. The FICO® score is used by the majority of lenders in the United States. There are different types of FICO® scoring models used for different types of consumer loans. A lender may use a different FICO® scoring model for a mortgage loan versus an auto loan or credit card account.

Your FICO® score is based on certain percentages. Thirty-five percent makes up your payment history. Thirty percent makes up the amount that you still owe on all outstanding accounts, number of accounts with balances, and how much of available credit is being used. Fifteen percent is made up of the length of your credit history. Ten percent is new credit, and ten percent is your credit mix (revolving credit lines aka credit cards and lines of credit and installment loans).

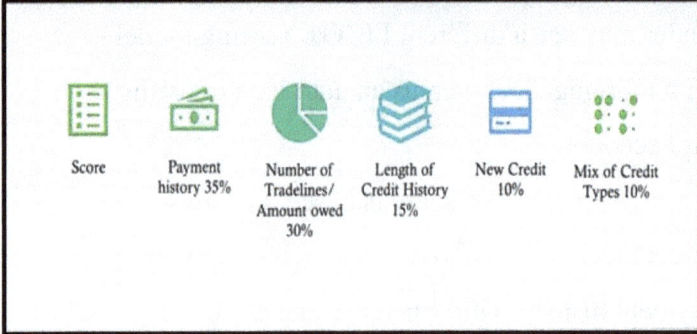

Credit History

| Score | Payment history 35% | Number of Tradelines/ Amount owed 30% | Length of Credit History 15% | New Credit 10% | Mix of Credit Types 10% |

FICO® scores range from 300 to 850. The lower the score, the worse your credit is. This indicates to the lender that you are a higher risk for defaulting on your obligation. The higher your credit score, the better your credit is which indicates that you are lower risk for default. Minimum acceptable FICO® scores are usually anywhere from 680 and higher for your conventional type mortgages. If you have other compensating factors such as a large down-payment, long job history, or a strong co-borrower, a lower FICO® score may be accepted. Most mortgages are approved with FICO® scores of 640 or higher.

If you do not have any credit, Fannie Mae and Freddie Mac have expanded their nontraditional credit procedures to take into consideration any borrowers that do not have "traditional trade lines". By traditional trade lines, I mean credit cards, signature loans, or other bank issued loans. "Nontraditional credit lines" may be cell phone bill payments, utility company payments, automobile insurance payments, life insurance policy payments, payments to local department stores or furniture stores or appliance stores, and any type of nontraditional credit payments that are being made but are not being reported on your credit bureaus. Experian has just introduced "Experian Boost™" to their scoring model to help increase or "boost" consumer credit scores. Keep in mind that this "boost" may not be applicable to mortgage lending credit score models.

Everyone has the right to receive one free credit report per year from each of the three major credit reporting agencies. You can get all reports and credit scores at one time per year at **www.annualcreditreport.com**.

Experian	(888) 397-3742	www.Experian.com
Equifax	(800) 685-1111	www.Equifax.com
Trans Union	(800) 916-8800	www.Transunion.com

When lenders order your credit scores, they are going to order all three credit bureaus at the same time and choose the middle of the three credit scores as your qualifying score. They will drop your lowest and highest score and use the middle credit score. If a borrower only has two credit scores that are reporting, the lender will use the lowest. If only one score is reporting, then that is the only score that they can and will use. Because errors are common within individual credit reports, it is wise to look at your credit reports *before applying* for your mortgage loan. Make sure that all information is reporting accurately!

You may use the Fair Credit Reporting Act to dispute any items on your credit bureau that are erroneous, that do not belong to you or that are not reporting accurately. Keep in mind, you may not apply for a mortgage while these items are under dispute. A mortgage underwriter will decline an application if there are trade lines that are still in dispute on a credit bureau. It is EXTREMELY important that your credit report is clean and ready to go *before you start* the application process, or you may be declined the first time you apply.

If you have credit issues, it is best to resolve them *before applying* for your mortgage loan. Some common mistakes that buyers make are:

1) Thinking that you can pay off old collection accounts to improve your credit score. After six months of inactivity, the impact of a derogatory statement lessens dramatically. Therefore, making a payment to an old collection makes that item active again and it can actually impact your credit score negatively. So, do not pay off old collection accounts unless the lender of that debt has agreed-**in writing**- to delete that item completely off of your credit bureau. Otherwise, you are spending money that you could use towards your down payment or closing costs, as well as possibly lowering your credit score.

2) Canceling old credit cards also will

negatively decrease your score. Since the length of credit history impacts 15% of your credit score, don't cancel old credit cards thinking that your credit score will increase because it will not! This will work <u>against</u> you.

3) Consolidating your debt will also trigger a lowered score until that loan is paid down to less than 30% of the total amount borrowed. Keep in mind that 30% of your score is based on the amount you owe on all of your accounts. New credit can negatively impact your credit score. Every time you apply for credit (a credit inquiry), points are deducted from your credit score. Acquiring new credit may indicate that you are not able to handle the debt that is already there. New accounts also lower the person's average account age which negatively impacts the score.

4) If your credit cards are maxed out, this is an indication that you cannot handle debt, and therefore, your mortgage may get declined.

5) Be careful if you start to shop your

credit card rates and open new accounts. Adding new accounts to your credit file will initially lower your score, but eventually your score will stabilize within 6 to 12 months. Be very aware of too many inquiries on your credit bureau because that too will be negatively looked at by the underwriter.

CREDIT TIPS

The best way to improve your credit score is to pay down- but DO NOT pay off- your existing credit accounts and keep all of the balances less than 30% of the actual credit line. For example, if you have a $1,000 credit line, you should keep a $300 or less balance on that card.

If you have slow or late payments, the greatest impact of late payments on a credit score happens during the first 30 to 60 days of being late. After that, the impact lessens. When a borrower makes a payment on such an account, it makes the account current and brings it to the top of the list. Again, basically the borrower has

put a spotlight on the poor payment history.
Keep in mind that payment history is 35% of
your score. If you want to raise your credit score,
keep making on time payments and stay beneath
30% of the approved credit limit. If you have
current credit issues while reading this book, it is
best to set a goal of applying for a mortgage in
the next 12 to 18 months while you make on-
time payments on your existing credit, as well as
pay down your credit limits. If you have
collections, it would be good to settle with the
creditor in exchange for deletion off of your
credit report *before* you apply for a mortgage.
This includes any open, unpaid judgments, back
child support, and/or eviction balances.

Be **aware** that FICO® has several different scoring models for various lending purposes such as home loans, auto loans, and credit cards. FICO® score 2, FICO® score 4, and FICO® score 5 are most often used by mortgage lenders when pulling your Experian, Equifax, and TransUnion credit bureaus.

Source:
www.ficoscore.com/education/#CreditBureaus

YOUR COLLATERAL

The final part of your mortgage process will be the property you are purchasing. Your lender will employ a licensed appraiser in your community to verify the market value of your purchase. You may verify appraisal district values online or in person at your county appraisal district office. You may also obtain a Broker Price Opinion (BPO) from one of your local Realtor® offices to verify the lender's appraiser's value.

BORROWER CHECKLIST

EMPLOYED

☐ 2 most recent paystubs with YTD figure

☐ 2 most recent years of filed Tax Returns with W-2's or 1099's

☐ 2 most recent months of bank statements

Savings accounts:

*Should show your down-payment and closing costs

Checking accounts:

*Should reflect your paycheck deposits

*Should be free of negative balances and/or bounced checks or overdraft fees

☐ Valid state-issued picture ID

SELF-EMPLOYED

☐ YTD Profit and Loss statement (CPA certified)

☐ 12 months most current bank statements (Personal AND Business accounts)

☐ 2 most recent years of filed Tax Returns with W-2's and 1099's

☐ Valid state-issued picture ID

SAMPLE GIFT LETTER

Gift Letter

I, _____, hereby certify that I/We given/will give a gift of
   _{DONOR NAME}

$ _____ to _____, my _____
   _{DOLLAR AMOUNT}   _{RECIPIENT}   _{RELATIONSHIP}

for the premises located at _____
                              _{PROPERTY ADDRESS}

on _____.
   _{DATE}

I/We certify that this is a bona fide gift and there is no obligation, expressed or implied, to repay this sum in cash or other services of any kind now or in the future.

I/We understand that this gift will require documentation, including proof I/We have given the gift from the account listed below, and proof that the funds have been received by the applicant or the applicant's attorney prior to settlement.

THE LENDER may confirm that the funds came from the account listed below:

Name of Depository or other Source: _____

Address of Same: _____

Account Number: _____

I/We Certify that the funds given to the applicant were not made available to the donor from any person or entity with an interest in the sale of the property including the seller, real estate agent, builder, loan officer, or any entity associated with them.

_____   _____
_{SIGNATURE OF DONOR}   _{TELEPHONE NUMBER}

_____
_{DONOR ADDRESS}

_____   _____
_{SIGNATURE OF RECIPIENT}   _{SIGNATURE OF RECIPIENT}

NECESSARY DOCUMENTATION FOR ALL LOANS (FANNIE MAE, FREDDIE MAC, FHA, USDA, VA):

1. Verification that gift funds were deposited into applicant's bank account (bank statement) or attorney trust account (escrow letter)
2. Donor's bank statement evidencing funds came from donor's account

WE ARE AWARE OF THE FOLLOWING:I/We fully understand that it is a Federal crime punishable by fine or imprisonment, or both, to knowingly make any false statements when applying for this mortgage, as applicable under the provision of Title 18, United States Code, Section 1014 and Section 1010.

HOW TO QUALIFY FOR CONVENTIONAL FINANCING

1. Calculate your GROSS monthly income.

2. Calculate all existing debts (all existing monthly debts reported on credit bureau + other monthly obligations such as child support/alimony—do **NOT** include utilities, cell phone payments, childcare, or things **NOT** reported on the credit bureau or court ordered).

3. For *conventional financing*, use the 28/36 ratios to find the maximum house payment your borrower can qualify for:

   a. 28% of Gross Monthly income is the maximum **HOUSE PAYMENT** Fannie Mae/Freddie Mac allows (PITI [Principal, Interest, Property Taxes, Insurance], + HOA monthly payment, and MIP/PMI)

   b. 36% of Gross Monthly income is HOUSE PAYMENT and all existing monthly debts reported on credit bureau + other court-ordered monthly obligations such as child support/alimony which known as **OVERALL DEBT RATIO**

4. Calculate BOTH ratios. (Gross monthly income * **.28** and Gross monthly income * **.36**)

5. Subtract all existing debts from the *overall debt ratio* (3b).

6. Use the lesser of 3(a) or (5) as your answer.

EXAMPLE:

Pamela makes $63,000 a year. She has credit card payments that are $110 each month, a car payment of $390 per month, and a student loan payment of $200 per month. Using conventional financing guidelines, what is the maximum house payment she can afford?

1. 63,000 / 12 = $**5250.00**/mo.
2. 110+390+200= $**700.00**/mo.
3. 5250*.28= $1,470   5250*.36=$**1,890**
4. 5250*.28= $1,470   5250*.36=$**1,890**
5. $1,890-$**700**= $1,190
6. $1,190 < $1,890; therefore, the correct answer is $1,190.

If she had no debt:
5. $1,890-**0**= $1,890
6. $1,470 < $1,890; therefore, the correct answer is $1,470.

THE LOAN APPLICATION

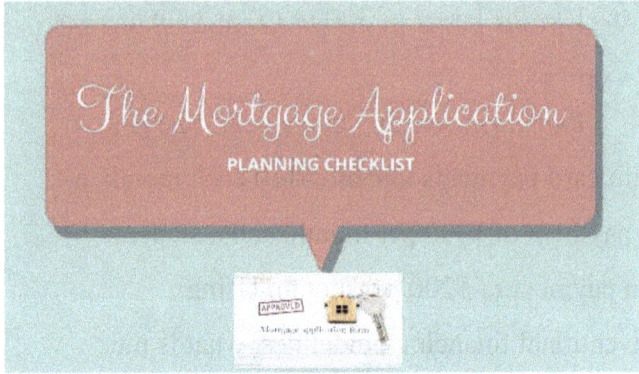

Shown in sections, you will see what questions your loan officer will ask you. Having this information *before* you apply will make your application process that much smoother. Take time to review this information and begin preparing your documentation to increase the likelihood of being approved the first time you apply. If you have a co-borrower, he or she will need to do the same.

BORROWER INFORMATION

Personal Information:
- Full name
- Social Security Number
- Date of Birth
- Citizenship

- Names of any co-borrowers
- Marital Status
- Number of Dependents
- Contact information (Phone number/Email address)
- Current address (Need 2-year history)
- Name of Employer (Need 2-year history)
- Gross Monthly Income (before deductions pay)
- Self-employment Income (if applicable)
- Income from any other sources

FINANCIAL INFORMATION

List of Assets:
- Checking/Savings/Money Market accounts
- Certificate of Deposit/Mutual Funds/Stocks/Stock Options/Bonds
- Retirement Account (ex: 401K, IRA, etc.)
- Trust Account
- Cash Value Life Insurance

List of Other Assets:
- Proceeds from Real Estate (investment property)
- Property to be sold on or before closing
- Proceeds from Sale of Non-Real Estate assets

List of Liabilities:
- Credit Cards
- Installment loans (car loan(s), student loan(s), etc.)
- Lease (non-real estate)
- Any open credit accounts

List of other liabilities and expenses:
- Alimony
- Child Support
- Separate maintenance

- Job related expenses

FINANCIAL INFORMATION (Real Estate)

Real Estate:
- Property you currently own
  - Address
  - Property Value
  - Occupancy (is it your primary residence, a second residence, a vacation property, an investment property?)
- Monthly rental income/expenses

LOAN and PROPERTY INFORMATION

- Loan amount
- Loan purpose (purchase, refinance, etc.)
- Property address
- Occupancy (primary residence, 2nd home, investment property)
- Will you use this property as residence and business (mixed-use)?
- Other new mortgage loans on the property you are buying or refinancing
  - Creditor name
  - Type of lien (first lien or subordinate lien)
  - Monthly payment
  - Loan amount
  - Other rental income on the property you are buying or refinancing (if applicable)
- Any gifts or grants you have been given or will receive for this loan (if applicable).

- Source(s) of any gifts or grants to be used for this transaction.

DECLARATIONS

- Will you occupy the property as your primary residence? If YES, have you had an ownership in another property in the last three years? If YES, what type of property and how did you hold title (self, jointly with spouse, jointly with another person?)
- If this is a Purchase Transaction, do you or your co-borrower have a family relationship or business affiliation with the seller?
- Are you borrowing any money for this real estate transaction (ex. Closing costs or down payment) from the seller or realtor?
- Have you or will you be applying for a mortgage loan on another property on or before closing on this loan that you have not disclosed?
- Have you or will you be applying for any new credit (installment loans, credit cards, etc.) on or before closing this transaction that has not been disclosed?
- Are you a co-signer or guarantor on any debt or loan that is not disclosed on this application?
- Are there any outstanding judgments against you?
- Are you currently delinquent or in default on a Federal debt?
- Are you currently a party to a lawsuit in which you could potentially have any personal financial liability?

- Have you conveyed title to any property in lieu of foreclosure in the past 7 years?
- Have you had any property foreclosed upon in the last 7 years?
- Have you declared bankruptcy within the past 7 years? (if yes, was it a Chapter 7, 11, 12, or 13?)
- Within the past 7 years, have you completed a pre-foreclosure sale or short sale whereby the property was sold to a 3rd party and the Lender agreed to accept less than the outstanding balance due?

ACKNOWLEDGEMENTS AND AGREEMENTS

I agree to, acknowledge, and represent the following:
- *The information provided in this application is true, accurate, and complete as of the date signed.*
- *If any information provided changes before the loan closes, I will provide the updated information.*
- *The terms of the contract used for this mortgage are true and accurate.*
- *Any intentional or negligent misrepresentation of information may result in civil liabilities and/or criminal penalties.*
- *The loan applied for will be used as security for the mortgage.*
- *Any appraisal or value of the property obtained by the Lender is for use by the Lender.*
- *The Lender may use electronic/paper records.*
- *The Lender or Other Loan Participants may report information about this account to credit bureaus.*
- *I authorize the Lender and Other Loan Participants to obtain, use, and share with each other, the loan*

*application and related loan information and
documentation.*

- *I authorize the Lender and Other Loan Participants
  to obtain, use, and share with each other, the
  consumer credit report on me and my tax return
  information.*
- *They may also verify any data contained in my
  consumer credit report along with other
  information supporting my loan application.*

MILITARY SERVICE

- *Did you (or your deceased spouse) ever serve, or
  are you currently serving in the United States
  Armed Forces?*
  *IF YES, provide information regarding length of
  service, and whether you are still active and your
  projected expiration date of service/tour.*

DEMOGRAPHIC INFORMATION

- Ethnicity
- Race
- Gender

LOAN ORIGINATOR INFORMATION

- Organization Name and Address
- NMLSR ID#
- State License #
- Loan Originator Name, NMLS#, State License #,
  Email address, Phone number

RESOURCES

Credit

www.AnnualCreditReport.com
www.Experian.com
www.Equifax.com
www.TransUnion.com
www.MyFico.com
www.CreditSesame
www.CreditKarma.com
www.ftc.gov/enforcement/statutes/fair-credit-reporting-act

Banking

www.BankRate.com
www.ChexSystem.com

Mortgage

www.HomeSteps.com
www.HomePath.com
www.HUD.gov
www.NMLSConsumerAccess.org

Realtor

www.Realtor.com

Get a free checklist here!
www.FreeGiftFromBrokerMelissa.com